9.95

The Joy of
Flowers

Stirling Macoboy

CHARTWELL
BOOKS INC.

For my friends
in Polynesia
who understand
the Joy of Flowers

Photographs
Page 1: Blue Waterlily
Nymphaea capensis var. zanzibariensis

Page 2: Orchid Cactus
Epiphyllum X 'Pink Nymph'

Published 1978 by Chartwell Books Inc.
A Division of Book Sales Inc.
110 Enterprise Avenue
Secaucus, New Jersey 07094

First published 1978 by Summit Books
Paul Hamlyn Pty Limited
176 South Creek Road, Dee Why West
NSW, Australia, 2099
©Copyright Paul Hamlyn Pty Limited 1978
Produced in Australia by the Publisher
Typeset in Australia by Terrey Hills Typesetters
Printed in Hong Kong

ISBN: 0 89009 201 X

Library of Congress
Catalog Card Number 78-51934

Contents

Kroměřížová

Introduction

'Flowers,' exclaimed the American preacher Henry Ward Beecher,
'... flowers are the sweetest things God ever made and forgot to
put a soul into ...'

The Reverend Beecher was fond of using simple, everyday images to introduce his fire and brimstone sermons; images that his congregation could visualize, and were likely to understand and love. Typically, he often chose flowers to strike a joyful chord in the minds of his listeners—for who among us has not at some time been overwhelmed by the beauty of some favourite or unfamiliar flower? Joy may lead to wonder, as we marvel for a moment at the sheer beauty lavished by nature in the creation of a purely functional object. For a flower, after all, needs only to be a plant's mechanism for reproduction of its species.

Might it not be, then, that flowers are intended as well to give us joy, by stimulating our sense of sight through form and colour; our sense of smell through the endless variety of scents and fragrances; our sense of touch through the lavish juxtaposition of textures and translucencies?

Alas, in these days of tension and crowding, we don't all have the space or the time any more to raise flowers for ourselves. But this in no way sets a limitation on our joy at discovering a new species—or on rediscovering a long lost friend of the floral world, whose heady fragrance reminds us of some childhood pleasure.

I still remember being given, as a child, a solitary orchid flower from a corsage worn by a family friend on some special occasion. I kept it for weeks in the ice-chest (no refrigeration then) and took it out for a few minutes of every day, just for the joy of looking at it.

But most of all, I store among the memories of my Tasmanian childhood the sight and scent of fields of purple-red Scabious (the Mourning Bride), naturalized in the long summer grass of a friend's house by the sea. I have not seen them in such quantity, or smelled them in such fragrance, at any time since.

My memories of favourite flowers are more numerous perhaps than most, for I have been fortunate enough to photograph them in climates, and at places, where each variety can be seen at its best.

No one person, anywhere, could grow all the flowers I have chosen to include in this book in a single garden. But flower lovers in every country will find some of their favourites included.

By showing them together, in a single volume, I hope to please not only those dedicated to following old favourites, but others who look for a special pleasure in the discovery of the rich and strange.

For there is a flower, somewhere, to suit every taste and every personality. Once again, I am indebted to the Reverend Beecher for his thoughts:

'Flowers have an expression of countenance as much as men or
animals. Some seem to smile; some have a sad expression; some are
pensive and diffident, others again are plain, honest and upright,
like the broad-faced sunflower and the hollyhock.'

Rosa 'Paul's Scarlet'

Roses, roses all the way...

'The Rose doth deserve the chief place among all floures whatsoever; being not only esteemed for his beauty, vertues, and his fragrant and odoriferous smell, but also because it is the honor and ornament of our English Scepter, as by the conjunction appeareth, in the writing of those two most Royall Houses of Lancaster and York.'

While it is painfully obvious, in that extract from John Gerard's Elizabethan *Herball* of 1597, that he was writing in the hope of gaining royal favour, the book is of inestimable value in telling us what flowers were actually grown in the days of good Queen Bess.

The rose was celebrated then as the most important of cultivated flowers: so it is today, and so it was 5000 years before our time.

The Chinese grew roses around 3000 B.C. Several millenia later, the Greeks had a word for them, *'Rhodos'*, and gave that name to the Mediterranean island where they grew to perfection. Greek poets Sappho and Anacreon hailed the rose as Queen of Flowers!

Later still, the Romans prized rose blooms for their fragrance, enjoying them at banquets as both a delicacy and a dedication to Venus, their goddess of love. Cleopatra spent over sixty pounds weight of gold to buy rose petals for the famous banquet where she seduced Mark Antony. They carpeted the decks of her galley twenty inches thick beneath a golden net.

Historian Pliny describes twelve varieties of rose that were cultivated in Rome. Some are still grown, but now take second place to the beauties raised by modern hybridists. New rose species introduced from Persia and India, from China and North America, brought with them yellow, pink, bronze and cerise colourings, and the continuous flowering habit we take so much for granted.

The ancients knew roses only as red or white, and could look forward to their blooming only at the height of summer.

As a reminder of man's own fleeting span on earth, they attracted much attention from Elizabethan poets like Robert Herrick ...

'Gather ye rosebuds while ye may,
Old time is still a-flying!
And this same flower that smiles today
Tomorrow will be dying.'

◁
The nineteenth century introduction of *Rosa multiflora* from Japan brought with it the gift of year-round bloom, and also bequeathed to modern roses a cluster-flowering habit. It became one parent of the *polyantha* roses and thus an ancestor of modern *floribundas*.

9

Species Roses

'The Rose looks fair, but fairer we it deem
For that sweet odour which doth in it live . . .'
                    Shakespeare

Individual characteristics of many different wild rose species have been blended to achieve the perfection of today's hybrid varieties. But sometimes the old species themselves are refreshing in their purity of colour, their richness of scent. Perhaps as a reaction against modern perfection, many home gardeners are seeking them out for today's gardens.

△
The rampant *Rosa gigantea* from Burma was a nineteenth century discovery that brought incredible vigour of growth into the blood of climbing roses. The Australian-raised 'Nancy Hayward' is of *gigantea* parentage, and perhaps the loveliest climber ever, with profuse four-inch single blooms of glowing carmine.

10

▷
Rosa cooperi was a Burmese introduction to influence modern
hybrid roses. This *cooperi* hybrid
was photographed at Malmaison,
Empress Joséphine's breathtaking
rose garden outside Paris.

▷
The 'Ramanas Rose', *Rosa rugosa*
was brought from China in the
mid-eighteenth century. It has
distinctive wrinkled leaves and a
suckering habit which is useful in
hedgemaking. The flowers are
often of a rich cerise or purple
shade. The *rugosa* hybrid 'F. J.
Grootendorst' was a sensation of
1918.

△
Rosa wichuraiana, the 'Rambler Rose', came from the Orient in 1891; its hybrid 'American Pillar' has been popular since 1902.

▷
Rosa foetida Persiana, the 'Persian Yellow Rose', brought with it in 1839 a fully double habit, the colour yellow and wonderful fragrance. This is its hybrid 'Agnes' of 1922.

Empress of the Roses

Rose by name (she was christened Joséphine Rose in Martinique) and a rose-lover by nature, Napoleon's first Empress created a garden outside Paris which became synonymous with roses.

No rose species was too obscure, no trouble or amount of money too great to bring it to Malmaison.

Even today, her garden is the Mecca of rose lovers. The three exquisite varieties on these two pages were photographed there.

△
Soft in colour, rich in perfume, 'Souvenir de Malmaison' is the perfect evocation of a royal rose garden.

◁
French hybridist Meilland's *flori-bunda* masterpiece is 'Sarabande', introduced in 1957. Throughout summer and autumn it continuously bears semi-double flowers of brilliant red, and in enormous clusters.

◁
The beautiful *floribunda* 'Manx Queen' was launched by rose breeder Alex Dickson in 1963. The golden-bronze flowers are tipped red, and there is a crimson flush to both stems and foliage.

The Floribundas

Modern *floribunda* roses with multiple blooms of medium size, are basically the result of much tedious crossing of the many-flowered dwarf *polyantha* roses, with the larger Hybrid Teas. The first (now forgotten) varieties appeared in 1924, but the flood gates opened after the Second World War to produce gorgeous bedding and cutting flowers like those on these pages.

△

*'I sometimes think
that never blows so red
The rose as where
some buried Caesar bled.'*

Omar Khayyam's verse comes to mind on viewing the gorgeous *floribunda* 'Alain', flowering on the site of Paris's grim Castle of Vincennes, a former Royal prison.

◁
'Dame Edith Helen', a vintage Hybrid Tea rose of 1926, was disappointing in European gardens but seems still to enjoy the Australian climate, producing perfect blooms year after year.

◁
'Emeraude d'Or', a stunning semi-double variety of the later 1960s, did not become popular outside Europe, where its red-edged golden blooms and decoratively ragged petal-edges caused a sensation.

'O Rose thou art sick!
The invisible worm
That flies in the night
Has found out thy bed
Of crimson joy,
And his dark secret love
Does thy life destroy.'
William Blake

▷
'What's in a name?'

Perhaps the loveliest of all Hybrid Tea roses, the internationally acclaimed 'Peace' first appeared in 1942 as 'Madame Meilland'. Basically cream and gold with pink-flushed edges, it has almost as many names as it has petals. 'Gloria Dei' and 'Gioia' are two others by which it is known.

▷
McGredy's Irish Rose 'Rubaiyat', a 1946 introduction, is still highly valued for mass bedding, producing splendid great flowers the colour of Ceylon rubies.

'My love is like a red red rose
That's newly sprung in June.'
Robbie Burns

◁

For a long time considered the most perfect Hybrid Tea rose ever raised, 'Perfekta', the 1957 masterpiece of German breeder Wilhelm Kordes, is in itself a direct offspring of the Dutch variety 'Spek's Yellow'.

◁

Tantau's 1960 introduction 'Super Star' brought a new colour into the Hybrid Tea palette—a brilliant vermilion orange. One of its four grandparents was the famous 'Peace'.

▷

A graphic illustration of the rose breeder's art shows in these three pictures. After his triumphant launching of 'Perfekta' (above), Wilhelm Kordes went one better and crossed it with rival breeder Tantau's 'Super Star' (below). The result, in 1964, a new Hybrid Tea rose with 'Perfekta's' shape, toning, and dark foliage—combined with the unusual ground colouring of 'Super Star'. He called it 'Konigin der Rosen' ('Queen of the Roses') and that is it on the page opposite.

◁

McGredy's Hybrid Tea rose 'Daily Sketch' was a show-stopper on its introduction in 1960. Very free-flowering, its many-petalled deep pink and silver flowers darken to a rich red as they age.

◁

The exquisite Hybrid Tea 'Lutèce' was raised by French grower Lathulle in 1965. Its lightly rippled petals form a most un-usual cup shape, revealing stamens of purest gold.

'They are not long,
the days of wine and roses!
Out of a misty dream
Our path emerges for a while,
then closes . . .'
Edward Dowson

△
Only a small part of the Tea rose colour range shows in this profuse
arrangement. Modern Hybrid Teas are of astonishingly varied
parentage. Their ancestors include the recurrently flowering single red
Rosa chinensis; *R. moschata*, the late-blooming cream 'Musk Rose'
which extends the flowering season; white *R. damascena* from the
Middle East; pink to red *R. gallica*, the European Wild rose;
R. foetida, the 'Austrian Briar' with single bronze flowers; and
R. foetida Persiana, a double yellow. True blues have eluded the
modern rose hybridists, but they are working on it.

Tulipomania

> 'But as to tell you of all the sorts of Tulipas . . . doth both passe my ability, and as I beleeve the skill of any other . . . besides this glory of variety in colors that these flowers have, they carry so stately and delightful a forme . . . that there is no Lady or Gentlewoman of any worth, that is not caught with this delight, or not delighted with these flowers.'

Thus in 1629 wrote John Parkinson, King's botanist to Charles I, in a foretaste of the enthusiasm for these stately bulbs which was to devastate Europe only a few years later.

Tulipomania (as it is sometimes called) has swept civilization at several times in history (although the flower was quite unknown to Shakespeare, who can usually be relied on as a diarist of floral taste in his day; and there is no apparent reference to it in classical mythology). In fact, the first recorded mention in Europe dates only from 1554, in the diary of a Holy Roman Emperor's ambassador to the Turkish Sultan. He recorded, in the vicinity of Constantinople,

> 'an abundance of flowers . . . which the Turks call tulipam [These] have little or no smell, but are admired for the beauty and variety of their colours.'

Five years later, Tulips were growing in the gardens of Vienna; within five decades a French devotee exchanged an entire brewery worth 30,000 francs, for a single rare bulb!

The Tulipomania swept into Holland (now that flower's spiritual home) where it became the centre of a crazy bout of speculation, based on the flower's habit of 'breaking' unpredictably into new and unusual colour variegations, which never revert. Soon, everyone with a pot or two was growing tulips, and waiting for the inevitable break to a new colour which could be sold to wealthy collectors. The crash came in 1637, when the collectors suddenly lost interest.

A century later, another tulip craze swept Turkey, though on a less commercial basis. Nobles throughout the land vied to outdo each other in displays of the beautiful flower which had been adopted as the official badge of the Turkish Imperial house.

Again, during the nineteenth century industrial revolution, the spectre of Tulipomania appeared in the North of England, but faded when the price of bulbs quickly outstripped the amateur gardeners' earnings.

Today, tulips are still admired for their dazzling beauty in late spring —but the fervour has faded.

> 'And where the tulip, following close behind
> The feet of Spring, her scarlet chalice rears,
> There Ferhad for the love of Shirin pined,
> Dyeing the desert red with his heart's tears.'
> _Persian Legend_

Cottage Tulip 'Marshal Haig'.

△
A recent development—the streaked gold and green beauty of *Tulipa viridiflora Praecox*, quite artificial in its unusual shape and colour.

◁
'Georgette', a brilliantly coloured mass of the popular *multiflora* tulip strain, bearing several flowers to a stem.

▷
Almost the elusive Black Tulip of Alexandre Dumas' novel? 'Queen of the Night', a dark maroon variety of the Darwin tulip.

△
More useful for cutting than
bedding, the curiously twisted and
torn Parrot Tulips are collectors'
favourites. Here, 'Orange Parrot'.

◁
Giants of the tulip family are
sumptuous 'Double Late'
varieties. Magnificent rose-pink
'Eros' may open five inches across.

▷
The unbelievable display of spring
tulips at Spalding in England
attracts tourists from all over the
world. Among the massed plant-
ings shown here are 'Halcro',
'Joanna' and the wonderful violet
'Silver Wedding'.

◁
'Triumph' tulips are early flowering varieties of medium height. 'Areola' is particularly eyecatching.

▷
'Sunkist'—a splendid golden tulip of the tall-growing 'Darwin' type, so greatly valued for late spring bedding.

▽
The open 'Lily-flowered' tulips have always been more popular in gardens of the Middle East—this is 'China Pink'.

Daisies ~ KOPRETINY
the eyes of God

'Myriads of Daisies have shone forth in flower
Near the lark's nest, and in their natural hour
Have passed away . . .'

Wordsworth was in the company of a thousand poets from all ages when he wrote (as he often did) of the humble daisy.

And yet perhaps not so very humble, for the English name has its origin in 'Deus Eyes'—the 'Eyes of God', from a medieval belief that the Almighty watched man's every move through the unwinking golden eyes of the omnipresent daisy flowers. The superstition probably had its origin in ancient sun worship, for daisies open to the sun's first rays and close at sunset. The Greek sun-god was Helios, whose name is remembered in the names of many daisy types: there are *Helianthus, Heliopsis, Helichrysum, Helipterum* and many more.

Daisies are probably mentioned more than any other flower in both folklore and literature, which is not really surprising since they make up the most numerous of all botanical families, the Compositae. And that is the clue to what daisies are all about: each daisy head is not a single flower, but a composite of tens, hundreds and even thousands of tiny simple flowers, each capable of separate fertilization and seed production. This composite head (which is usually called the eye or disc) is surrounded by one or more rows of *rays* or modified petals, which are common to the whole flower cluster. These are often brilliantly coloured.

With all these eye-catching qualities, few daisies have any need for perfume to attract their fertilizing visitors, so most of them have either no scent at all, or just a plain common or garden *smell*, not always attractive.

There are over 13,000 recorded daisy species, and their most common habitat is in the great grasslands and prairies of the world.

There is an intriguing sidelight to daisy lore in the old game 'She loves me, she loves me not', recited by many a frustrated swain to his breathless wide-eyed lady love. What will the daisy say? she wonders. The wry truth of the matter is that the daisy will make whatever point the cunning lover wishes to get across. Provided he starts off with 'she loves me', the game will always finish up the same way, for over 95 per cent of daisy flowers have an odd number of petals. And doesn't she wish she knew *that* before it was too late!

◁
The 'Marguerite' or 'Paris Daisy' (*Chrysanthemum frutescens*) was introduced from the Canary Islands in the sixteenth century. They were almost certainly named for Queen Marguerite de Valois, in whose Paris garden they grew about 1600.

△
There is an old English saying:

> *'Summer has come when you can set foot on seven daisies all at once'*

and in cold climates the opening golden daisy eyes are always a cheerful sign after a long, hard winter. This is the wild 'English Daisy', *Bellis perennis*, and it has pink and red varieties.

▷ AKSAMITNÍK

The sunny 'Marigold' or 'Gold Daisy' has been a favourite in Western gardens since the Middle Ages. Always popular with poets, it is the subject of a rather sad little verse written by King Charles I when awaiting his execution:

> *'The Marigold observes the Sun More than my Subjects me have done . . .'*

The charming 'Swan River Daisy' is a West Australian annual that should be seen more often—particularly in its native land. Easy to grow from broadcast seeds, it flowers in every imaginable combination of blue, mauve and white—sometimes with gold eyes, sometimes black. Its botanical name is *Brachycome*.

◁ KOKARDA

Gaillardia is the botanists' name for these showy blood-coloured daisies with ruby eyes. Native to the western prairies of North America, they have attracted the popular name 'Indian Blanket', both from their primitive colours, and from their softly grey-furred leaves.

◁ TŘÍPATKA

Also native to North America, but from cooler woodland areas, are the glorious *Rudbeckias* or 'Gloriosa Daisies'. Black cone-shaped eyes, and sparse rays of red, gold and bronze in many pattern combinations have brought them a place in perennial borders throughout the world.

▷ NERENKA

Arctotis are a feature in dry areas of the South African veldt from spring to autumn. Their colours seem to flow in soft waves away from the composite disc—just like the waves of colour in eastern skies at dawn. And so they are popularly called 'Aurora Daisies' after the Roman Dawn Goddess Aurora.

▷ USTÁLKA

The Spanish conquistadores first
noticed *Zinnias* in the elaborate
gardens of the Emperor Mocte-
zuma. They were customarily
watered with human blood, of
which there was no shortage in
that barbaric kingdom. Less spectacular than the technicoloured
varieties one sees in modern parks
is dwarf *Zinnia linearis*. These
were at one time called 'Brazilian
Marigold', but only because some-
one got their continents mixed up.

◁ TURAN

Erigeron are found on all northern continents, but particularly in cooler parts of North America. Tinted in a subdued range of blues and mauves, they are sometimes known as 'Quaker Daisies'. *Erigeron* differ from other daisies by having two or more rows of rays or petals surrounding the massed yellow florets of the eye.

▷ STARČEK

Senecio or 'Groundsels' are the largest daisy group with over 1500 species. They are found all over the globe, and the feature that sets them apart from other daisies is the greyish hair on many parts of the plant. Their botanical name comes from *senex*, Latin for an old man. The 'Old Man Daisy' *Senecio laxifolius* is a sprawling New Zealand shrub.

▷

The 'Livingstone Daisy' is one of nature's mimics. Not really a daisy at all, it is a South African succulent that has somehow developed flowers that look and act like the real thing. Botanically it is called *Dorotheanthus* after England's Queen Sophia Dorothea, with the specific name *bellidiformis*, meaning 'flowers like a daisy'.

If South Africa could name a daisy after the Dawn Goddess Aurora, it was a sure bet that some taxonomist would remember her mythological boyfriend, Tithonus—and so he did. *Tithonia* is the name given to a small genus of red and orange daisies from Mexico. More usually, they are known as Mexican Sunflowers, and you'll find them in warm climate gardens.

◁ SLUNEČNICE

In spite of their brief adoption by Oscar Wilde and English aesthetes of the late nineteenth century, the gigantic *Helianthus* or 'Sun-flowers' still hold their heads high above other garden flowers. As well they might; for they were once worshipped by the Incas of Peru as living representations of their Sun God.

▷ SMIL - SLAMĚNKA

The 'Paper Daisies', *Helichrysum*, are found on all continents except the Americas. Australia alone has more than a hundred species of which *H. bracteatum* has become popular throughout the world. Its disc of golden flowerets is surrounded by a rustling ring of brightly coloured bracts which feel exactly like elaborate paper decorations. Picked, the flowers last for months.

Proteas ~ the honey flowers

Wheel of Fire

◁

This stunning Protead from Queensland coastal forests has become popular throughout warm countries of the world. Its shining lobed leaves are decorative any time of year, and the flower clusters appear in autumn, often directly from the trunk and branches. These consist of a number of tubular two-inch flowers arranged like the spokes of a wheel. As the individual flowers turn scarlet, each splits into four segments, revealing a golden column, and the entire blossom cluster comes to resemble a gaudy medieval crown.

Of the many remarkable personalities in ancient Greek mythology, none had a more remarkable appearance than Proteus, son of the mighty sea-god Poseidon and an Egyptian Queen. A whole series of appearances in fact. He had the power of assuming any shape he chose in order to avoid mortals who would take advantage of his gift of prophecy. Proteus had complete knowledge of past, present and future—but could never voluntarily reveal his secrets. The poor fellow had to be surprised, bound and tortured into revelation. This was almost harder on his would-be captors than on him, for he might appear at any time as a tree, a serpent, a lion or even as fire or water. But if his captor could see through the disguise and bind him fast, the god would be forced to resume his proper shape and give a truthful answer to any question put.

It was this gift of unlimited shape-changing which suggested the generic name *Protea* to botanists classifying a newly discovered group of South African plants. These had a most variable appearance and became a sensation among eighteenth century plant collectors. Taxonomists then placed them in a new botanical family which they called Proteaceae, which included about fifty other closely related genera of plants from various warm (and once connected) parts of the southern hemisphere: over 1000 plants in all. *Leucadendron* and *Leucospermum* from South Africa; *Embothrium* from South America; and a dazzling array of Australian native plants including *Banksia, Dryandra, Grevillea, Hakea, Isopogon, Lambertia, Macadamia, Petrophila, Stenocarpus* and *Telopea*, the 'Waratah'.

All of these bear spectacular flower heads of great size. These are rich in honey and attractive to birds and bees. They vary from small shrubs to giant trees; and although most of them do have certain facets of appearance in common the most obvious similarity between them is their dissimilarity, both to each other, and to all other plants.

The Africans

◁

One of the most stunning colour combinations among flowers is produced by South Africa's 'Black Protea', *Protea neriifolia*. These splendid five-inch flower heads are enclosed in overlapping bracts of deep salmon with furry black tips; the whole is covered with silver, silky hair. Both flowers and oleander-like leaves last for weeks when cut.

◁

The gigantic flowers of the King Protea may reach a foot in diameter, yet appear on a plant rarely above waist height. Variable in colour, the dome-shaped mass of florets may be white or silver grey—the surrounding bracts pale golden-pink or crimson. One flower head surrounded by its strange paddle-shaped leaves makes a decorative indoor accent for months.

▷

Possibly the most spectacular of South Africa's Proteads is the fragile *Leucospermum tottum* or 'Firewheel Pincushion'. Each head contains a mass of individual orange flowers which split open and roll back into a compact cushion. Each flower then reveals a vividly coloured 'pin' or style which shades from lime green through orange and pink to cyclamen. Each of these styles bends to one side, and in the mass they resemble a revolving catherine wheel.

The Australians

◁

A mature Silky Oak in full bloom
is a sight never forgotten, and a
source of amazement to those who
know it only as a fast-growing but
flowerless indoor plant. Every twig
and branch tip seems covered with
a double row of rich golden-
orange flowers, rather like a
tightly curled toothbrush.
Grevillea robusta is its botanical
name, and it may grow to a
hundred feet in a favoured area.

◁

A common spring sight in the
bushland of Australia's east coast
are the delicate Spider Flowers,
Grevillea punicea. Every flower
cluster consists of many tubular
scarlet blossoms which roll back
their petals, each revealing a
single club-tipped style. It is these
curved styles which give the
flowers their spidery appearance
as they move in every passing
breeze.

▷
Remarkable is the only word
which describes the 'Sea Urchin
Flower' *Hakea laurina*, most
interesting of yet another Protead
genus. A native of Western Australia, it is widely grown as a
decorative shrub in the Mediterranean area and in southern California and New Zealand. The eye-
catching flower clusters appear in
early winter, each resembling a
perfectly round crimson pincushion, stuck all over with pale
cream pins. The blooms have a
delicate fragrance.

▷
Less commonly seen than their
gaudier Protead cousins, *Petrophila* have a delicate beauty of
their own. Commonly known as
'Drumsticks', and found in rough,
rocky areas of Australia (*Petrophila* means rock-lover), these
tough little shrubs produce a compact cone-shaped mass of flower
buds which develop into loose,
shaggy heads of soft furry flowers,
like pink velvet dipped in soot.
Individual blooms split to reveal
gold stamens.

More Australians

◁

The extraordinarily complex structure of many *Banksia* flower heads is illustrated in this close-up of the 'Hairpin Honeysuckle', *Banksia spinulosa*, a common plant in the hills to the west of Sydney. The neat rows of felty beige flowers are almost obscured by masses of bronze to purple styles, each bent to the shape of a hairpin. Bees adore the native Honeysuckles.

◁

Banksias are named for Sir Joseph Banks who discovered them on his first day in Australia with Cook, in 1770. The 'Coastal Honeysuckle' *Banksia integrifolia* was almost certainly the species he saw. Flower-spikes of this handsome, dark-leafed tree are tall, six-sided, bottlebrush-shaped structures of delicate greenish gold. Each flower opens to reveal a silky style of pale cream which gives the fully opened cluster a soft, fluffy effect.

◁
Yet another beautiful Protead genus, *Dryandra*, is well represented by this lovely flower, *Dryandra nobilis*. The showy blooms consist of a dense cone of downy golden flower tubes. These roll back to reveal needle-like styles that tangle with each other like a birds' nest of spun sugar—a startling contrast to the viciously saw-toothed leaves. Dryandras are found only in Western Australia.

△
Six-inch domes of coral-scarlet glowing in the forest depths mark the whereabouts of 'Waratah', the state flower of New South Wales. Its botanical name *Telopea* comes from a Greek word meaning 'seen from afar', in reference to the effect of these magnificent composite blooms—each consisting of many tubular flowers surrounded by a row of light crimson bracts. Waratah signals the peak of spring in New South Wales. The blooms cut well and last for weeks in water, a typical Protead characteristic.

Frangipani ~ PLUMERIA
the flower and the man

The frangipani (or *Plumeria* to use its botanical name) may well be the only flower to be named after a perfume, rather than the other way around.

It is said that a sybaritic seventeenth century Italian, Count Frangipani, developed and was fond of using an unique and heavy perfume, the composition of which was a mystery. When *Plumerias* were introduced many years later, their natural fragrance bore an uncanny resemblance to the Count's expensive scent, so they were called—Frangipani flower! But it may just be that the mystery perfume was made from the flowers themselves, for their Mexican homeland had already been settled for almost a century when the count was born.

The same gentleman is said to have been responsible for a delectable European dessert, Frangipane Cream, enjoyed as much for its fragrance as its flavour. This is compounded, among other things, of vanilla, almonds, kirsch liqueur, apricot jam and pistachio nuts. When these are blended, they do produce a fragrance which may remind some people of the frangipani flowers.

Some say the dessert was named after the flower, others, vice versa. The dispute will probably never be settled, for almost every variety of frangipani has a different perfume. This variation in scent is one of the ways to identify the parentage of an individual variety, others being the shape of the leaves and the colouring of the flowers.

Frangipanis hybridize naturally and indiscriminately, and seedlings are rarely true to the parent plant, which must be propagated by cuttings.

Flower lovers familiar only with the common cream and yellow *Plumeria* may even be surprised to learn that there are other colours, but in fact the varieties are almost without number. I have seen and photographed over sixty myself. A few cultivars have been named, and all of them are the result of crossing several of the five recognized species. These species are:

P. acuminata: cream and yellow flowers, hairy flower stalks, pale green pointed leaves.

P. alba: small white and yellow flowers, smooth stalks, paddle-shaped leaves.

P. bahamensis: white flowers, smooth stalks, narrow, dark leaves.

P. obtusa: large rounded white flowers, smooth stalks, dark evergreen leaves with rounded tips.

P. rubra: red flowers on hairy stalks. Shorter, more rounded leaves.

All species grow into trees twenty feet and more in height.

◁
To gardeners in many parts of the world, the name 'Frangipani' suggests only simple cream and yellow flowers with a diameter of two inches or so. Lovely as they are, they can scarcely compare with some of the gorgeous tropical hybrids like this ruffled raspberry beauty at Honolulu's Foster Gardens.

FRANGIPANI

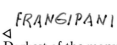

◁
Darkest of the many red
Plumerias, the wonderful variety
'Scott Pratt' produces blooms of
intense crimson, marked with
black. Its buds and flower stalks
are very nearly black, and even
the leaves are suffused with a
deep maroon shade.

◁
In Australia and nearby Pacific
areas, you may see a cream
Plumeria variety with elongated,
twisted petals flushed with gold
and pink. Its perfume is so rich
and hard to place, it is often
called 'Fruit Salad'.

▷
Largest of the many frangipanis in cultivation is the Hawaiian 'Daisy Wilcox', in which the short-stemmed floppy flowers may reach five inches in diameter. So large are the delicate salmon pink petals that they tend to overlap both themselves and other flowers.

▷
'Orange Fire' is the most vivid of all the *Plumeria* hybrids, and I have seen it only in older gardens of Tahiti. Its parentage is unknown, and its colouring of scarlet, orange and rich egg-yellow most unusual. The perfume is rather cloying.

◁
The rare and beautiful Hawaiian *Plumeria* 'Madame Poni' is unique in both the shape and the colour of its flowers. The bent petals have a curious 'gull wing' effect, and are sharply pointed— the flowers are a soft gold, marked with green and crimson. Each flower is four inches in diameter.

▽
'Emma Bryant' is a popular garden variety all over the Pacific area. The orange-centred flowers are a deep cerise pink with much paler reverses. The perfume is very heavy, and 'Emma Bryant' is probably a colour variation of the original *Plumeria rubra* species.

▷ This popular and cheerfully coloured Hawaiian *Plumeria* variety has been named 'Postman'. Its petals are rich orange-yellow and cerise, and the cream reverses are rolled over to give a distinctly spiral effect. Like many of the red hybrids, it has a rather sickly perfume.

▷ 'Singapore White' is not a variety, but an entirely different botanical species of *Plumeria*—*P. obtusa*. Its leaves are a very dark green, blunt-ended and wider near the tip than the base. The flowers too have blunt-ended petals. They are white, not cream, with a rich yellow centre, and their perfume is breathtaking. The foliage of 'Singapore White' tends to be evergreen in tropical climates.

Campanulas ~ ZVONKY
singing the blues

◁   ZVONEK
The beautiful 'Peach-leaf Campanula', *Campanula persicifolia*,
has been found growing wild right
across Europe and northern Asia
—even in sheltered parts of north
Africa. Its nodding, shallow bells
in every shade of blue, and even
white, have brought it favour as a
garden flower since the sixteenth
century.

'Emerald tufts, with flowers of purple, blue and white.'

Those nine words were apparently Shakespeare's only reference to
the great host of bellflower species found wild all over Europe and in
many parts of Asia.

There are around 250 of them, all useful in gardens (particularly
where the soil is chalky) for they provide the elusive shades of blue so
often missing in other flowers. Their botanical name *Campanula* means
'little bell' and almost all of them have bell-shaped flowers—or at least
they do if you use a little imagination. Many of them also have charming
old-fashioned popular names like 'Bats in the Belfry', 'Canterbury Bells',
'Venus' Looking-glass', 'Chimney Bellflower', 'Corn Violet', 'Bluebells
of Scotland' and 'Harebell'.

There are annual, biennial and perennial species among them, and
they vary from tiny creeping groundcovers to tall-growing woodland
plants six feet and more in height. There are even some African and
Hawaiian species within the family Campanulaceae which are classed as
trees, but you won't find them in any garden.

◁

Campanula latifolia is one of the
more popular garden species, a
native of cool, moist woodland
areas from England to Kashmir.
Its long, tubular bellflowers hang
loosely from a tall stem.

The 'Chinese Bellflower' *Platyco-don* grows wild in northern China, Siberia and Japan, but has been a favourite in Western gardens for about two centuries. It was once classed as a true campanula, but now is placed in a genus of its own. The leaves are toothed like holly, and the wonderful blue flowers may be three inches in diameter. *Platycodon* dies right back to its roots each winter.

▷
Arguably the rarest flower in the world, you will never find *Apetahia raiatiensis* in cultivation anywhere. It grows only in hidden places at the top of Temehani, a mountain on the sacred Polynesian island Ra'iatea, and has resisted all attempts to grow it elsewhere. It is the only species of the Campanulaceae family with a rather unique habit. Each dawn, plump green buds open with an audible pop, splitting right down one side as they become five-petalled half-flowers, very fragrant. The native name is Tiare Apetahi—'the one-sided flower'.

▷   ZVONEK
The 'Milky Bellflower' *Campanula lactiflora* is native to the Caucasus, but has been tamed in European gardens for about 150 years. In shady places, the milky-blue or white flowers appear throughout the summer on tall five-foot stems.

◁   ZVONEK
The dwarf Bellflower *C. carpatica* blooms in many parts of eastern Europe at the height of summer. The flowers are open and shaped more like a shallow cup than a bell.

Poppies ~ beautiful and deadly

'The poppy is painted glass; it never glows so brightly as when the sun shines through it. Wherever it is seen—against the light or with the light—always it is a flame, and warms the wind like a blown ruby.... When the flower opens, it seems a deliverance from torture; the two imprisoning green leaves are shaken to the ground, and the aggrieved corolla smoothes itself in the sun, and comforts itself as it can, but remains visibly crushed and hurt to the end of its days.'

So wrote the nineteenth century critic John Ruskin in a memorable evocation of these gorgeous flowers. Probably, though, he would have known only the common Corn Poppy, *Papaver rhoeas*, scornfully dismissed as 'Red Weed' by European farmers who fight it as an annual scourge among their crops. But the red poppy has survived since classical times, when Somnus, the god of sleep created it (according to legend) to calm the earth-goddess Ceres after her labours in the fields, and enable her to rest.

And that, in an appropriately soothing way, introduces an aspect of poppy culture about which we should not wax so joyful—all 450 or so species of the botanical family Papaveraceae carry a white milky sap which has narcotic and even deadly properties. The sixteenth century botanist Gerard observed:

'It mitigateth all kinds of paines, but it leaveth behind it oftentimes a mischiefe woorse than the disease it selfe.'

Yes, from this juice of a million poppies is extracted first opium, and then by refinement, morphine and heroin.

During Europe's industrial revolution, laudanum, a light dilution of opium, was used by the working classes to lighten their cares; in our own century an innocuously named 'Syrup of Poppies' was used to quieten fractious infants. Today, the perils of heroin addiction are daily reported in the press, and in Asia, millions slave in secret to raise the deadly flowers for export to the drug-ridden cultures of the West.

'... Not poppy, nor mandragora
Nor all the drowsy syrups of the world
Shall ever medecine thee to that sweet sleep
Which thou ownd'st yesterday ...'
                              Shakespeare

◁ SLUNCOVKA

There's always been 'gold in them thar hills' of southern California. Each year, after the spring rains, a million Eschscholzias erupt into a blaze of gold which can be seen for miles. For this reason, they say, the state was first named 'Tierra del Fuego' (Land of Fire) by Spanish seamen cruising off the Sunshine State. Many natural colour varieties have been identified.

But still we grow them for their beauty.

◁ MÁKY
The gaily coloured 'Shirley Poppies' were raised by a patient clergyman in England about a century ago, using as a starting point a single white-edged flower noticed among a field of scarlet corn poppies. Careful re-selection led to the colour range we know today—every shade from white to red, plain and variegated—but without a trace of the original corn poppy black in either petal or stamen.

△ MÁKY
Since the First World War a symbol of remembrance, the Corn Poppy *Papaver rhoeas* is the original poppy that 'blew in Flanders fields'— and for that matter, in fields all over Europe and much of the East. Its petals might be made of scarlet satin— with or without the brilliant black markings that reflect the blue of the sky.

◁

The 'Golden West' received its name from fields of the breathtaking but scentless California Poppy. *Eschscholzia californica* was called by Spanish missionaries 'Calce de Oro'—after the mythical Holy Grail. Unlike other poppy relatives, the leaves are feathery and a delicate blue grey. The flower bud is protected by a long, smooth cap, which pops off in one piece.

▷

This gay little dwarf from Japan (and other parts of temperate East Asia) is alone in its own division of the poppy family. *Hylomecon japonicum* grows from a rhizome, and the leaves look more like those of a strawberry than a poppy, but the flowers are unmistakeable. Rich, golden yellow and four-petalled, with a mass of green stamens.

▷

Common among the rocky foothills of Welsh mountains, pretty *Meconopsis cambrica*, 'the Bastard Poppy' was for centuries believed to be the sole member of its genus: then came the discovery of blue-flowered relatives in Tibet (see page 66), and in this century a whole horde of cousins has been introduced to cultivation from remote parts of the Himalayas.

'Poppies procureth sleepe.'

A beautifully fringed and fluted form of the Opium Poppy, *Papaver somniferum*, photographed in Queensland. This species is cultivated not only for its beauty and narcotic content, but also for its seeds which are used worldwide for cooking purposes. Rather at odds with their beauty, Opium Poppies have a somewhat offensive smell.

◁

Opium Poppies are often depicted in old Dutch flower paintings, and have been in cultivation for centuries. The original species seems to have been mauve or purple; but over the years, gardeners have developed additional colours in single and fully double flowers, some with curled, divided or fringed petals. This old form known as the 'Paeony Flowered Poppy' was photographed in a field near Berriedale, New South Wales. The smooth grey buds and leaves are typical of the species.

▷

One of the most popular cut flowers in winter, the 'Iceland Poppy' comes from sub-arctic regions of Asia. The original species was a charming lemon-yellow with greenish centre, but hybridists have followed the taste of the times by developing a wide range of colours, both garish and pastel. The flowers are held on tall hairy stems, well above the rosette of much-divided leaves.

▷
'A miracle of loveliness' is one botanical writer's description of the gorgeous 'Matilija Poppy'. 'Fried-egg Flower' is another less elegant but quite understandable local name for this stunning perennial poppy from southern California. Difficult to propagate and establish in cultivated gardens, it appears to thrive on neglect in dry, sandy soil. Unlike most poppies, *Romneya* normally has five or even six petals, seeming to be made of snow-white crinkled crepe. The centre boss of golden stamens exudes a rich, delicious perfume and each individual flower may reach nine inches in diameter.

△
Showiest of the family are the giant 'Oriental Poppies' with crepe-finished blooms six or eight inches in diameter. Originally vivid orange with black markings, hybridists have crossed them with related species to produce a wide range of more acceptable colours. *Papaver orientale* is essentially a perennial plant for the cooler climate.

◁
A garden sensation between the two World Wars, the 'Blue Poppy of Tibet', *Meconopsis betonicifolia*, is less often seen these days; though plants can occasionally be bought at nurseries in mountain areas. A pity, for it is not difficult to grow in the dappled shade of a woodsy garden with really good drainage. It does not pick well, but imagine those enormous sky blue flowers among your magnolias!

Lilies of the field

'Consider the lilies of the field, how they grow; they toil not, neither do they spin: yet I say unto you, that even Solomon in all his glory was not arrayed like one of these.'

That part of Jesus' sermon on the mount is frequently quoted as the ultimate statement on the regal beauty of lilies. But in fact both modern botanists and classical scholars believe the King James' Bible contains a mis-translation.

The only lily known to antiquity was a small white species, and anyway, the Hebrew word used in the earliest manuscripts of the sermon was *'Shushan'* which means any brightly coloured flower. The Gospel's 'Lilies of the Field' are much more likely to have been *Ranunculi* or *Anemones*. Both of these are native to and plentiful in Palestine, and either of them could more aptly be compared to the gaudiness of royal raiment.

The word 'lily' comes from the Persian *'laleh'*, and even today is used indiscriminately in the common names of many flowers which are not lilies in the botanical sense. The only *true* lilies are eighty-odd species of *Lilium*, some of which have been in cultivation for nearly 5000 years. They are a superb genus of highly perfumed bulbous plants found *only* on the three continents of the northern hemisphere and nearby islands. They grow mostly in rich and well-drained woodland areas.

The *Liliums* in turn are members of the much larger botanical family Liliaceae, most of which grow from corms, rhizomes or some other form of bulbous root system. These are *not* limited to the northern hemisphere, and several representative species from Australia and Africa are illustrated in this section of the book.

The lily of classical times was *L. candidum*, the 'White Lily'. Now known as the 'Madonna Lily' it held religious significance for the Greeks and Romans as the symbol of Juno, mother of the gods, from whose milk it was believed to have sprung in all its white perfection.

'Better and sweeter are they than all the other plants,' wrote the ninth century monk Strabo, *'and rightly called the flower of flowers. Yes, roses and lilies, the one for virginity with no sordid toil, no warmth of love, but the glow of their own sweet scent, which spreads further than their rival roses . . .'*

A peculiarity here is that even today, nobody has succeeded in extracting and fixing that delicious sweet scent for perfumery.

◁
Nature alone could never have produced the gorgeous lily across the page, for its parentage includes *Lilium* species from three separate continents. It is called 'Destiny' and was raised in Oregon in the United States.

◁

A giant among lilies—and yet, not quite a lily! Taxonomists are still arguing whether the wonderful flower at left is a real *Lilium* or should be called a *Cardiocrinum*, which merely means a lily with heart-shaped leaves. The *big* differences are that it grows to ten feet, and the football-size main bulb dies after flowering, leaving offsets to bloom another year. Because of its size, it is obviously suited only to large woodsy gardens.

▷LILIE

Most recently discovered of the major lilies, the superb *Lilium regale* (or 'Royal Lily') was discovered in a remote valley between Tibet and China in 1904. It is the perfect answer for gardeners who just 'can't grow lilies', a wonderful creamy-white with pink reverses to the petals and an almost overpowering perfume.

LILIE

Pink perfection! Some of today's most spectacular garden lilies are the 'Oriental Hybrids' of which 'Adventure' is a superb example. These are the result of a painstaking three-way cross between a trio of Japanese species: *Lilium speciosum* (above right) from which they inherit reflexed petals and perfume; *L. auratum* (below), from which they draw size of bloom, and *L. japonicum*, from which comes the wonderful pink colour and single flowering habit.

▷

Lilium speciosum, a traditional lily of Japanese gardens was introduced to the West in 1832, and its pink flushed varieties are often sold as 'Pink Tiger Lilies'. The reflexed flowers, which are usually centred in lime green, are deliciously fragrant and borne on tall, stiff stems, ideal for cutting.

▷ LILIE ZLATÁ

The legendary 'Gold-Rayed Lily' of Japan (*Lilium auratum*) finally bloomed in the West in 1862, but has always been finicky and prone to virus disease. The gold-banded summer flowers, up to nine inches in diameter, open in large numbers on stems taller than a tall man. The pollen stains badly, and is often removed if the flowers are to be cut for indoors. There are many named varieties, from purest white to darkest crimson in colour. The one at right is 'Gold Lady'.

LILIE

◁

Among the first man-made lilies
to win universal acclaim were the
'Mid Century Hybrids' developed
from the old-fashioned orange
Tiger Lily. 'Enchantment' is
probably the most popular of
these.

▷

Lilium X 'Discovery' is a modern
hybrid developed from the purple-
flowered 'Turk's Cap Lily' (*L.
martagon*) of the Middle East.
From this parent it inherits the
downward facing flowers with
strongly reflexed petals.

▷

Discovered in California in 1875,
the 'Panther Lily', *Lilium parda-
linum* has adapted well to woodland gardens throughout the
world. As many as twenty of the
strongly reflexed flowers may be
found on stems up to eight feet in
height. Each bloom is curiously
coloured in orange and purple,
more like a nursery panther than
a real one.

LILIE
Lilies of the south

Though all true *Liliums* are
found only in the northern
hemisphere, there are many
equally spectacular members
of the Liliaceae family south
of the equator. All those
illustrated unfortunately lack
the rich lily perfume of the
north.

◁

The 'Climbing Lily' *Littonia*, is a
most unusual plant from the
Transvaal: growing from a tuber,
it has adapted to climbing by the
development of fine tendrils at the
tips of its leaves. The rich golden
bell-flowers open at the top of a
six-foot stem.

◁

The 'Gloriosa Lily' climbs in the
same fashion as *Littonia*, and
sprawls into a dense covering
over nearby shrubs and fallen logs.
There it produces gorgeous hang-
ing flowers of red and gold, like
exquisite tropical insects. It is
native to Uganda and known
botanically as *Gloriosa roths-
childiana*.

▷

Blandfordia nobilis is Australia's
best-known member of the lily
family. It blooms in midsummer
in coastal bushlands of the eastern
states, when it is sold widely in
Sydney flower stalls as 'Christmas
Bells'.

Lilies of the lake LEKNÍNY

*'Now folds the lily all her sweetness up,
And slips into the bosom of the lake;'*

With these somewhat cloying words, Tennyson, the Victorian poet laureate perhaps over-romanticized the habits of the spectacular waterlily family, the Nymphaeaceae. Fold their petals up they certainly do—some in the evening, some at the approach of dawn, according to species—but I have never seen one slip into the bosom of the lake, and yet I consider myself fairly observant.

Most of us, however, would agree with Lord Tennyson that they are remarkably attractive flowers. All species of the relatively small family are to be found in temperate and tropical climates right around the globe. All of them grow in still or sluggishly moving water, with their roots deeply twined into the mud of the waterbed. All bear flowers that are recognizably similar, though beyond that, their growth habits vary widely.

The true waterlilies, *Nymphaea*, are named of course for the water-nymphs of classical mythology. They have hollow stems and leaves which actually float on the water surface. Varieties from temperate climes float their flowers on the water as well—while those from the tropics hold their blossoms on tall stems, high above the surface. The most famous of these is the Sacred Lotus of Egyptian art and mythology, which opens its white flowers only at night; but most species in today's water-gardens are day flowerers—with hybrid varieties in shades of pink, blue, apricot, red and yellow.

The closely related Sacred Lotus of India, China and Japan is classed botanically as a *Nelumbo* (which is its name in the Sinhalese dialect of Sri Lanka). *Nelumbo* grows from buried rhizomes, like many irises, and holds both flowers and leaves on tall stems well above water level.

There are several other genera of waterlilies not seen much in cultivation outside botanic gardens. One is the giant *Victoria amazonica* from tropical Brazil, with leaves so vast they can bear the weight of a small human without sinking. Another group are called *Nuphar* (which is the Arabian word for waterlily). These invariably have yellow flowers and are found wild in America, Europe and Asia.

All waterlily species are perfumed, their fragrances varying from mild to overpowering.

◁

Nymphaea stellata is one of the commonest of warm-climate waterlilies, holding its star-shaped flowers well above the water. It is commonly the palest blue, but there are Star Lily varieties in white, pink and even red-violet. It is native to India and South East Asia.

△
*'Where drooping lotus-flowers,
    distilling balm,
Dream by the drowsy streamlets
    sleep hath crowned . . .'*

Almost artificial in their waxy
perfection, most waterlily flowers
open wide at sunrise, close at dusk.
But a few of the tropical species
bloom at night, suffusing a sweet,
heavy fragrance to attract night-
flying insects.

▷
'Escarboucle' is the name given by
the French to this glowing hybrid
waterlily. *'Escarboucle'* means
Ruby, and what other description
do you need for this translucent,
splendid flower?

LEKNÍNY

80

△ LEKNÍNY

An American species, the charming Golden or Mexican Waterlily
(*Nymphaea flava*), grows best in
a warmer climate with mild
winters. The blooms are of only
medium size, the leaves have
rippled edges.

LEKNÍNY

◁
Away from temperate climes, the
waterlilies are more vividly
coloured and hold their flowers
high above the water. Many
tropical species are blue, ranging
from palest powder blue through
azure almost to violet. The leaves
of African *Nymphaea capensis* are
distinctly toothed, the golden
stamens tipped with a matching
blue. (See also illustration on
page 1.)

◁
In Australia's tropical north and
in nearby parts of South East Asia
the blue 'Native Waterlily' blooms
throughout the year. The flowers
are exquisitely perfumed, but
difficult to use indoors because
they close as daylight fades.
Florists sometimes retard this habit
by spraying the centre of the open
flower with hair spray.

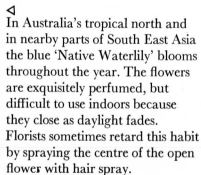

The Jewel in the Lotus
△

Great blue-green umbrella leaves held high above the still water—
sheltering among them, a pale rose-tipped flower of unparalleled
delicacy, all of ten inches in diameter. That is *Nelumbo nucifera*, the
Sacred Lotus of Buddhism, and a giant of the waterlily family. To
Buddhists, this glorious blossom proves that virtue and purity can
triumph in spite of the world's wickedness. This because the Lotus rises
from foul mud through polluted waters and yet produces a miracle of
perfection in its flower. The Buddha himself is often shown seated on a
golden Lotus.

Perfuming the air

◁

*'Full many a flower is born to
 blush unseen,
 And waste its fragrance on the
 desert air,'*

wrote Gray, the poet. Might he
have been speaking, I wonder, of
the pale and beautiful cactus
known as 'Belle de Nuit'? A giant
among flowers, often the size of a
soup plate, it opens in the dark of
summer nights (never before nine
o'clock in my garden), suffusing
the air with waves of exotic
perfume. For an hour or two, the
great, snowy blooms glow faintly
in the moonlight, then, before
dawn's first rays, it dies—shrink-
ing and twisting away from the
light, its perfume spent. Botanists
call it *Epiphyllum oxypetalum*,
but I prefer the French name, or
its translation 'Beauty of the
Night'.

*'To throw a perfume on the violet,' wrote Shakespeare, 'is
wasteful and ridiculous excess.'*

Some might believe the violet would be lovely enough without
perfume, but the overwhelming majority of flower lovers value fragrance
above all.

Shakespeare's friend and contemporary, Francis Bacon, wrote:

*'Because the breath of flowers is far sweeter in the air (where it
comes and goes, like the warbling of Music) than in the hand,
therefore nothing is more fit for that delight, than to know
what be the flowers and plants that do best perfume the air.'*

Many popular perfume flowers are already shown elsewhere in this
book, but fragrance, more than any other flower quality, is subjective,
and often related in the mind to an individual bloom's colour, shape and
texture—even to some pleasant past association with that flower. The
Chinese in general abominate the *Plumeria* (frangipani), calling it 'the
Graveyard Flower' because it is often planted in such situations. Some
adore the aromatic spicy smell of lavender or rosemary. To many, used
to the gentle fragrances of the European garden, the liberal perfumes of
the tropic Tuberose and Y'lang Y'lang seem overpowering and vulgar.

Not all memorable perfumes are produced by the flower itself. In the
case of lavender, peppermint, rosemary, violet and geranium, the
volatile oil which pleases our senses is most concentrated in the leaves.
In the citrus family it is in the skin of the fruits as well as in the flowers.
In aniseed and nutmeg and almonds it is in the seed. Cinnamon, cassia,
cedar and camphor come from the wood and bark of their respective
plants. Cloves are from flower buds, patchouli from a stem, ginger from
roots.

But all of these fragrances make life more pleasant in different degrees
to different people, and few of us would quarrel today with the thoughts
of Abraham Cowley, writing in the seventeenth century:

*'Who that has Reason, and his Smell,
Would not among Roses and Jasmin dwell,
Rather than all his spirits choak
With exhalations of Durt and Smoak . . .'*

85

PHILADELPHUS JASMÍN

◁

'Perfumes, in fact, rarely come from the flowers whose names they bear . . . with the exception of the inimitable Jasmine, which is impossible to counterfeit.'

Joris Huysmans, 1884
(*Jasminum polyanthum*)

▷

A century before Christ, there was a Roman Consul, Lucius Lucullus, who scandalized the eternal city with his free spending and love of private luxury. His name is quite appropriately kept alive in the richly perfumed, luxurious blooms of the *Luculia*, a fussy, obstinate shrub from the Himalayas which produces one of the most perfect fragrances in the garden—if it will condescend to share it with you. Be sure to pick your *Luculia* lavishly, for it blooms only on new season's growth.

◁

'The flower of sweetest smell is shy and lowly,'

observed the poet, and the legendary Tiare Tahiti makes truth of his observation. A wide-spreading, low growing shrub; its seven-petalled flowers open late in the day, often hidden beneath the notably shiny leaves. The shape and texture are perfect, the perfume magnificent, for this joy of the dark-eyed Vahines is a true Gardenia, *Gardenia taitiensis*.

◁ VOSKOVKA
'For he on honey-dew hath fed,
And drunk the milk of Paradise.'

Coleridge's exotic lines from
'Kubla Khan' seem to reflect the
richness of the 'Beautiful Honey
Flower', shown several times
actual size in our picture. *Hoya
bella*, as science calls it, is a small,
weeping Asian plant, rich in perfume and so loaded with sticky
honey-dew it positively drips.

◁ '*I shall return in Springtime, with the Violets,*'

were Napoleon's parting words as he left his beloved France for exile. And return he did, making time to lay a posy of his favourite flower on the grave of Joséphine, his favourite wife. *Viola odorata,* the 'Sweet Violet', which legend says first sprang beneath the shadow of Orpheus' lute, grows wild in Europe and has been celebrated throughout history. Once the state flower of Athens, later the symbol of Napoleon, it was also the favourite of England's Queen Alexandra, who introduced the fashion of wearing an entire bunch of them pinned to her costume. 'What is charm?' wrote Marion Crawford in 1909. 'It is what the violet has and the Camellia has not . . .' We don't have to agree with him all the way to appreciate the fragrance of this shy and shaded harbinger of spring.

◁ '*Lavender groweth in Spain aboundantly, in many places so wilde, and little regarded, that many have gone, and abiden there to distill the oyle therof,*'

wrote Parkinson, the Elizabethan herbalist, proving that the delicate perfume of this Mediterranean herb was as greatly valued in his day as in our own. There are many (myself among them) who still keep a sachet of dried lavender in the linen cupboard to impart a cooling fragrance to the bedlinen on hot summer nights. The fragrance is particularly long lasting, the sachet I use was made up by my grandmother over forty years ago.

▷ CHÝR-FIALA

Old-fashioned wallflowers or *Cheiranthus* grow so readily that they pop up in the most unlikely places, even crevices of walls, once they are established. Neither colourful nor showy, there is a special reason for their popularity:

> *'The wallflower on each rifted*
> *   rock,*
> *From liberal blossom shall*
> *   breathe down*
> *its fragrance . . .'*

enthused the poet Moir, while the botanical chatterbox Parkinson noted,

> *'the sweetnesse of the*
> *flowers causeth them to be*
> *generally used in Nosegays and*
> *to deck up houses . . .'*

They were called 'Heart's Ease' in Elizabethan times.

▷

> *'Bid her steal into the pleachéd*
> *   bower,*
> *Where honeysuckles, ripen'd by*
> *the sun*
> *Forbid the sun to enter.'*

The poet was also an observant gardener, for these delightful vines prefer shade for their rampant growth and then produce their deliciously fragrant flowers high up in the sunlight. This is particularly so with the Giant ZIMOLEZ Burmese Honeysuckle, *Lonicera hildebrandiana*, whose honey-rich golden blossoms may reach six inches in length.

Winter's joy~ KAMÉLIE
Camellias

'*Silent the garden*
Where the Camellia tree
Opens its whiteness.'

Even in English translation, the delicate 'haiku' verse of Japanese poet Onitsura evokes the ghostly presence of these elegant flowers in a winter landscape. Buds unfolding, leaves sparkling in the sunlight, spent blooms falling to carpet the bare, cold ground.

Evergreen, flowering when other shrubs have gone to winter rest, camellias are favoured world wide for their waxen flowers that glow in the short-day sun and seem almost to arrange themselves for indoor use.

In temperate areas, a winter garden without camellias may seem unthinkable; but for all that they are relative newcomers outside Asia.

Though the story may be apocryphal, it is generally claimed that the first camellias to leave the East (apart from dried botanical specimens) arrived in London aboard an East India Company ship in 1792. And that as a result, this most perfect of flowers was introduced to Western gardens by accident. Accident, because the plants were believed to be specimens of the colourless *Camellia sinensis*, the dried leaves of which are the tea of commerce, the tea we drink.

Tea had just become the rage of Europe, being imported at great expense from China, a country where Western contacts were limited by Imperial decree to a few fringe ports. The East India Company, possessing a virtual monopoly on Eastern trade with England, had bribed Chinese officials to obtain seedlings of the precious tea plant, which they hoped to propagate in England for their Indian estates. But the wily Chinese outsmarted the traders and substituted plants of the more decorative *C. japonica*, the leaves of which were useless for teamaking.

But oh! its flowers! The Company's loss was the gain of gardeners everywhere, and the waxy red or white flowers became a botanical sensation almost overnight, being introduced within a few years to climatically suitable areas of Europe, America and Australia. Cultivation of the tea plant itself was almost forgotten, as the rush to import new flowering varieties from Asia began.

And many variations there were, in quiet temple gardens of China, Korea and Japan. Even since the Second World War, the most gorgeous and fragrant of all camellias, the *reticulatas*, have been discovered among the misty hills and moist valleys of China's Yunnan province. See some of them on page 98.

◁
Unfamiliar even to many camellia lovers is the resplendent *Camellia granthamiana*, a new species discovered as recently as 1955 on a sheltered hillside of the New Territories of Hong Kong. One plant only was found, but this wonderful flower has propagated well and is now flourishing in many parts of the world. Each creamy-white blossom is almost six inches across, with eight petals surrounding a boss of drooping orange-gold stamens. The cushiony leaves have deeply impressed veins, and the branches a weeping habit.

◁ Large for a *sasanqua*, the blooms of striking *'Navajo'* may be up to three inches across. The petals are a rich rose red in colour, fading gradually to cream at the centre, where they surround a superb cluster of stamens with a slight petaloid effect.

▷ A typically shaped *sasanqua* *'Setsugekka'* has textured petals of remarkable delicacy: pure white, waxy and daintily fluted. In fact the English translation of its Japanese name is 'Wavy White'. *Setsugekka* may be trained as a charming potted plant.

▷ Notable particularly for its weeping habit, the *sasanqua* *'Red Willow'* bears delicate semi-double flowers among its willow-like foliage in early winter. With careful training, it can become a sensational bonsai, its foliage remaining decorative year-round.

▷ All camellias are inclined to throw 'sports', which must be propagated by grafting. Sometimes these appear on an existing plant—sometimes in the form of a seedling like this charmingly fringed unnamed sport of *C. sasanqua* variety *'Cheri'*.

▷ Sometimes listed as a variety of *C. hiemalis* (a related species), *'Showa no Sakae'* or *'Glory'* is the nearest to a fully double of the many *sasanquas*. Its soft pink flowers have the shape and appearance of a rose.

▷ The exquisitely formed semi-double *'Jennifer Susan'* has rippled rose-pink petals with darker edges and curled tips. The stamens form an open powderpuff of gold, and the foliage is a dark green, brilliantly glossy.

The Sasanquas

The fragile-flowered *sasanqua* camellias are descended from an autumn-blooming Japanese species. Fast growing, they luxuriate in full sun and flower profusely from late summer to mid-winter. The six varieties illustrated were photographed at the E.G. Waterhouse National Camellia Garden at Caringbah, New South Wales.

The Japonicas

Hybrids of *Camellia japonica* (originally from Japan and Korea) are by far the most commonly grown world wide. There are at least four thousand varieties in cultivation, flowering some time from earliest winter to late spring.

◁

In the curious way that camellias have, this splendid sport (later named '*The Czar*') appeared in a garden in Melbourne, Victoria, in 1913, though on what plant is not recorded. Like the Czars of old Russia, it is indeed magnificently arrayed. Glowing red and semi-double, its petals are swirled and deeply veined, surrounding a mass of gold-tasselled stamens. Each flower may be four inches in diameter.

◁

In Japanese, '*Hatsu-zakura*' means 'first cherry blossom'; it is a highly appropriate name for a camellia which may bloom as early as autumn in mild climates. The large four-inch flowers are a deep warm rose and extremely variable. The five large petals may be cupped or reflexed; the gold tipped stamens may be plain or bear a mass of petaloids like a tightly curled chrysanthemum. It originated in Japan, where it is also called '*Daitairin*'.

'A Camellia
dropped down into still water
of a deep, dark well.'
                    BUSŌN
                    1716-1783

▷

'Kelvingtoniana', 'Gigantea',
'Gaiety', 'Kaiser Wilhelm'—the
many names of this gorgeous
Camellia japonica variety bear
witness to its popularity in many
lands. It is said to have appeared
first in a European garden in the
1840s and is seen in old gardens
everywhere. The flowers are
marbled deep pink and white with
a cushion of similarly variegated
petaloids. The foliage is dark and
lustrous.

▷

Introduced in America in 1949,
this large-flowered japonica
variety 'R. L. Wheeler' is particularly striking. Deep rose-pink
in colour and semi-double, its
heavy outer petals are turned
backward, and centred with a
bouquet of fluted smaller petals
and gold-tipped stamens; each
flower may be five inches across.
The leaves have a pronounced
toothed effect on their edges.

More Japonicas

◁

In bud, or freshly opened, the blossoms of *C. japonica* variety *'Cho-cho-san'* (Madame Butterfly) have an extraordinary perfection and delicacy—but alas, like the operatic heroine after whom they were named, they are highly vulnerable, and after a short time, inclined to break up and drop. Semi-double and concave in shape, the flowers are palest pink, their stamens tipped with brownish gold. It was introduced to the West in the 1930s.

▷

There are many aficionados of the camellia who believe *'Guilio Nucchio'* to be the finest *japonica* hybrid raised yet. Its flowers are as large as any *reticulata* camellia— up to six inches across—semi-double and of a rich coral rose shade, almost red. The petals are irregular and waved, surrounding a mixture of tall petaloids and golden stamens. The flowers have a superb velvety texture, and the lush green foliage is of a weeping habit. It is California bred.

◁

Although its single flowers are faintly scented and tinted a delicious strawberry icecream shade, this curious variety of *Camellia japonica* is prized for its unique foliage, in which every dark shiny leaf is divided and twisted at the tip, like the tail of a fancy goldfish. And that is what the Japanese call it—*'Kingyo Tsubaki'*, the 'Goldfish Camellia'. Elsewhere it is also known as *'Quercifolia'* (Oakleafed) or *'Fishtail'*. But the Japanese name is surely the most appropriate.

The Reticulatas KAMÉLIE

The species *C. reticulata* was introduced to Western gardens in the 1930s from remote provinces of China. Named varieties appeared only after the Second World War. Their foliage is sparse, the perfume delightful and the flowers themselves may reach six inches in diameter, like the cyclamen-toned *'Flower Girl'* (above), a hybrid between the *reticulata* and *sasanqua* species.

▽
'Francie L', a startling oriental red *reticulata* hybrid was introduced to the United States only in 1964.

KAMÉLIE
Some other species

Beyond the popular camellias shown in the preceding pages, there are around ninety additional wild species. Few of these are seen in cultivation, though they are occasionally used in hybridization.

▷
Most delicate of flowers, the *C. vernalis* variety '*Star above Star*', from Japan, is almost transparent, shading from white to palest lavender. It is certainly related to some of the *sasanqua* hybrids.

▷
'*Showa wabisuki*' is a tiny single white camellia with magnificent dark foliage. It is classed in the species *C. dunnii*, whose origin is unknown.

◁
A true *reticulata* variety from China's Yunnan province, '*Mouchang*' is a picture in ruffled salmon-pink with bronze-tipped stamens.

▷
Found in a temple garden of southern China, the rare species *Camellia heterophylla* now has several hybrids including dainty '*Barbara Hillier*'.

Roses of China ~ IBIŠEK
the Hibiscus

It was Linnaeus, inventor of our present system of botanical nomenclature, who first used the name 'Rose of China', in the eighteenth century, when he christened these fantastic tropical flowers *Hibiscus rosa-sinensis*. The name 'Hibiscus' itself was Greek, and formerly used for the related and similar wild European marsh mallow. The origin of the name is obscure, but probably an adaptation of 'Ibis' the birds which feed on the young mallow plants in nature.

But even Linnaeus could be wrong. He believed the hibiscus came from China itself—for they were certainly grown there at the time of the earliest European contacts—but modern botanical thought inclines to the Indian Ocean area as the more likely original home. Species sufficiently compatible to cross are found in East Africa, Madagascar and Malaysia—and also throughout the Pacific Islands to which they may have been carried by the Polynesians. Other species native to the Middle East and China itself do not cross with *H. rosa-sinensis*.

At any rate the popular types we all know certainly reach their full glory only in tropical and sub-tropical gardens. In fully tropic zones they flower throughout the year; in cooler areas in summer only, the flowers peaking in size with the advent of the autumn rains.

Early hibiscus introductions to the West were sometimes known as 'Flower of a Day'—for that is generally their life span. But as the result of modern hybridizing, certain varieties may last as long as three days, either on the plant or when picked early in the morning. Place them in water or just lay them about the house, it makes no difference to their lasting qualities.

The spiritual, if not the actual home of the ornamental hibiscus is Hawaii, whose state flower and emblem it has become. The Hawaiian islands have three native species of their own, and these have been crossed with at least thirty-three other species introduced from different tropic areas to produce the stunning hybrids we know today.

> *'Flowers of such remarkable size and hue,*
> *Flowers such as Eden never knew'*

is a verse that most aptly describes them.

At one time, there were over 5000 named varieties grown in Hawaii, but the Islanders became bored with them, and now reserve their enthusiasm for other flowers. Currently gardeners in Australia and Tahiti would seem to be in the lead developing new colours. In the latter country, as in most of Polynesia, the single red hibiscus was considered sacred, for according to legend it was made by Tane, the creator god, from the ruddy face of man. The old religion has gone, but the memory lingers: in many parts of the South Seas, a hibiscus flower worn behind the right ear means 'I seek a lover'—behind the left 'I am spoken for'. Wear two and you could be considered promiscuous.

◁
Hybrid hibiscus from the tropics have a mixed parentage from many lands, flower in many colour combinations. Included in our picture are popular cultivars including *'Surfrider'*, *'Elegance'*, *'Haleakala'*, *'Catavki'*, and *'Golden Belle'*, some of which may reach ten inches in diameter.

◁

Hibiscus 'Apple Blossom' is a fast growing hybrid of several Eastern and Hawaiian species, much planted as a street decoration in warm climates, where it reaches tree size. It is particularly profuse in blooming, but the crimson-centred soft pink flowers, alas, last only one day before they close and drop.

◁

'Oh lost green paradise,
Were the roses redder there
Than they bloom other where?'

Was Christina Rossetti thinking,
when she wrote, of the glowing
colour found in so many of the
Roses of China? Gigantic hybrid
'Mary Forbes' seems to include
every shade of red from scarlet to
cyclamen.

▷

'Therese' they call this spectacular
soft-yellow bloom with ruffled,
irregularly shaped petals—the
centre shading to a soft strawberry pink. The flowers appear in
large numbers throughout the hot
weather, growing larger as the
temperature climbs.

▷

Nameless but eminently nameable,
this barbarically coloured hibiscus
was developed by Tahitian
hybridist Jacques Rentier. Red,
orange, pink combine in the
reflexed ruffled petals, the whole
irregularly splashed and rayed
with vivid yellow.

◁ Remarkable for its tremendous size and elongated twisted petals, the stunningly coloured *'Elegance'* has another quality not often found among the *rosa-sinensis* hybrids. The individual flowers will last three full days, whether placed in water or not.

▷ One of the earliest species to reach the West (in 1690), the Chinese *Hibiscus mutabilis* is less tropical in its needs than others, and quite different in its growth and appearance. The leaves are heart-shaped and hairy, the three-inch flowers (which may be single or double) open pure white at dawn, fade to pink by midday and a deep reddish shade before they close at dusk, never to re-open. In the southern United States it is known affectionately as the 'Confederate Rose'.

▷ Sole representative of shrubby hibiscuses in cool climate gardens, the 'Rose of Sharon', *H. syriacus* carries generally three-lobed leaves and is deciduous. Flowers of the original species are single, lilac blue with red centres, but there are modern hybrids in white and palest pink, some semi-double. *H. syriacus* does not cross with the tropical species.

◁
The Hau or 'Tree Hibiscus' is a
common seaside plant throughout
the tropics, where its golden
flowers turn bronze and finally
crimson in the course of several
days. A tree decked in blossom
of many colours is a veritable
Joseph's Coat. The individual
blooms, as they drop, are often
carried out to sea, and may be
found floating many miles from
land. Again, it does not cross with
other species.

▷
No longer classed as a true
member of the genus, Australia's
'Blue Hibiscus' has been re-
christened *Alyogyne huegelii*. It
bears dark, scented, five-lobed
leaves, often quite woolly, and
exquisite five-petalled flowers with
a delicate mauve-blue tint. These
last several days before closing. In
a dry, warm climate, the flowers
may reach five inches in diameter.

◁
East Africa is home to the delicate
'Skeleton Hibiscus' or 'Coral
Hibiscus', a spidery long-stemmed
flower with curled and reflexed
petals of intense red. In Hawaii it
has been crossed with other
species, lending its luxuriant
ruffled effect to many hybrids.

◁
Almost identical to the Asiatic and Pacific hibiscuses, the closely related *Malvaviscus arboreus* (or Turk's Cap) varies in two important respects. Firstly, it is native to the American tropics, and secondly the beautiful drooping flowers never open! This causes a deal of confusion to newly settled garden-lovers in tropical climates, who just cannot understand why their hibiscus plant does not behave like those in the garden next door.

Flowers of passion

In spite of their torrid appearance, there is nothing romantic about the passion which named these tropic beauties! They were called *Flos passionis*—'the Flower of the Passion of our Lord'—by Spanish Jesuit missionaries who discovered them in the jungles of South America. These zealous churchmen were amazed to observe in one blossom so many reminders of the Passion or suffering of Christ—and eagerly used the common flowers to illustrate graphic lectures on the Crucifixion to potential native converts.

The five petals and five sepals were said to symbolize the ten apostles who remained faithful to the end (Judas the betrayer, and Peter who thrice denied his Lord, being conveniently omitted. The showy corona of course, was said to symbolize either the Crown of Thorns, or the halo, depending on the situation. The five stamens represented the five wounds, the three styles the three nails used on the cross.

In addition, the plant's climbing tendrils were said to represent the cords or scourges, and the handsome palmate leaves to remind us of the hands of Christ's tormentors. White passionflower species were used to symbolize purity; the blue-coloured flowers the heavenly vault; and the scarlet blossoms the blood shed by our Lord. Finally, observing that the flower conveniently bloomed for three days, they decided to link this with Christ's three-year ministry.

All passionflowers are tropical in origin, and bear fruit only in favourable locations.

◁ MUČENKA
From tropical South America, *Passiflora coccinea*, surely the most eye-catching of the many passionflowers. Each magnificent bloom may be up to four inches in diameter and has both petals and sepals lined with velvety scarlet. The filaments of the corona shade from purple to a pinkish white.

◁
Most commonly seen of the 500-odd passionflower varieties, *P. caerulea* is popular as a garden climber even in Europe, for it is native to cooler areas. The three-inch summer flowers are pinkish white in colour, while the corona shades from white to purple. Flowers are followed by brilliant but sour orange fruits, which persist to autumn.

Amaryllis ~ ZORNICE
lilies of the Autumn

'Shed no tear—O shed no tear!
The flower will bloom another year.
Weep no more—O weep no more!
Young buds sleep in the root's white core.'

Keats reveals himself, in this verse, a more observant botanist than most of our famous poets, several of whom have been caught wanting during research for this book.

The majority of the family Amaryllidaceae die right away after flowering, in a manner that has been known to engender panic in the novice gardener. But all is well, the next season's flower buds are there, fully developed in the heart of the bulb—although we do not recommend you reassure yourself by bisecting it!

There are some 700 species included in the family. Many of them closely resemble the Liliaceae in general appearance, and were once classed in the same family. One notable amaryllid species is still named *Crinum*, which comes from *krinon* the ancient Greek word for lily. But to the botanist, there are distinct differences which made a reclassification necessary.

In amaryllids, for instance, the ovary or seed receptacle is situated well below the junction of petals and stamens. The majority of species are found in tropical and subtropical areas, and flower during the dry season, in autumn and winter. Mostly they grow from large bulbs, but some grow from running roots or rhizomes.

Taxonomists are still at work on this family, and some are known by different names in different lands. The *Hippeastrum* for instance, is still more generally known in the United States as an *Amaryllis*, whereas in the rest of the world that genus is now limited to the one species, *Amaryllis belladonna*, the 'Belladonna Lily' or 'Naked Lady'.

Many amaryllids are quite amenable to pot culture, and will flower beautifully for years without disturbance. Their flowers include some of the largest and most spectacular among all plants. In addition to the few species illustrated here, the family Amaryllidaceae also includes such popular bulbous plants are *Agave, Alstroemeria, Bomarea, Brunsvigia, Cyrtanthus, Doryanthes, Eucharis, Galanthus, Habranthus, Haemanthus, Hypoxis, Ismene, Leucojum, Macropidia, Narcissus, Sternbergia, Vallota* and *Zephyranthes.*

◁
The 'Golden Spider Lily' *Lycoris aurea*, was named for Lycoris the Golden, a celebrated actress in ancient Rome, who became the mistress of Mark Antony and later of the poet Gallus. Perhaps like its somewhat tarnished name-sake, this gaudy flower is most spectacular in the autumn of its year. It is from China.

◁

'The tuberose, with her silvery light,
That in the gardens of Malay is call'd the Mistress of the Night . . .'

Poet Thomas Moore wrote many charming botanical verses, but after the above I am inclined to regard all of them with suspicion. The tuberose (*Polianthes tuberosa*) was discovered in Mexico in 1629, and although it is one of the Amaryllidaceae is certainly not a lover of Malaysian type climates. Nor, I believe, does it flower at night. Poor Thomas, you can't win them all!

◁ ΚΡΊΝ

Crinums (from the Greek *krinon*, a lily) are an important genus in this family, found in warm areas of all the world's continents, generally by rivers or the sea coast. There is very little doubt that their wide global distribution is partly due to these preferred locations, for the large seeds float. *C. asiaticum*, known unpleasantly as the 'Asian Poison Lily' is like most *Crinums* evergreen. It flowers continually in the tropics, where the blooms are used for personal adornment. The bulbs are used in Chinese medicine as an emetic.

▷ *'Their colour is the most perfect Red,'* wrote eighteenth century botanist John Hill, *'and they are spangled all over as it were with Gold. Nature, not to lavish her Treasures upon one Flower, has denied this Fragrance. One sense is fully satisfied with it, and even more, for in the Sun the Eyes do ache to look upon it.'*

Nerine sarniensis was long known as the 'Guernsey Lily' from its prevalence on that island in the seventeenth century. Only when it was rediscovered in South Africa did botanists realize it had floated ashore in Guernsey from a Dutch shipwreck. The name *Nerine* is singularly appropriate for a flower cast up from the sea: the Nerines or Nereids were, in classic mythology, sea nymphs, the fifty daughters of sea-god Nereus by an incestuous marriage.

▷ The 'Filmy Lily', *Hymenocallis littoralis* is one of about forty species of beautiful amaryllids—all save one from South America. They take their botanical name from Hymen, the Greek god of marriage, and son to Apollo by one of the Muses. He is described in legends as a youth of such delicate beauty that he might be taken for a girl, which seems appropriate. *Hymenocallis* species are generally pure white and very fragrant. They can be distinguished from other tropical amaryllids by their daffodil-like trumpet.

◁

Mercifully abbreviated from the name of German botanist J. H. von Sprekelsen, the *Sprekelia* is a Mexican amaryllid. It can be identified in old Aztec manuscripts, from which it receives its popular name 'Aztec Lily'. *Sprekelias* can be grown in pots and flowered several times a year, merely by withholding water for several months after the blood-red flowers have died down. These, in shape, are extraordinarily reminiscent of the heraldic 'Fleur de Lys'.

▷

Alas for Amaryllis, the Greek beauty whose name was once immortalized in a very large genus of bulbs indeed! One by one they have been stolen away, renamed and recompartmented by the heartless taxonomists, until she has but one namesake left. *Amaryllis belladonna*, the 'Beautiful Lady' or 'Naked Lady' sends up bare flower stems from the earth in autumn, to break into a riot of gorgeous pink lily-flowers with an equally gorgeous perfume.

◁

These popular orange amaryllids were named *Clivea* after the maiden name of a nineteenth century Duchess of Northumberland. Whether the lady ever grew them is unrecorded, but she did live about the time they were first brought from their native Natal in South Africa. With dense evergreen foliage and winter flowers, they have long been popular in neglected parts of the garden, and are best left there, for they have no perfume and exude an unpleasant yellow-green sap when cut.

◁

Calostemma is Greek for 'Beautiful Crown', although the Greeks themselves never knew these lovely amaryllids from warmer parts of Australia. The name refers to the curious way the gold stamens are united at the base, giving the appearance of a tiny gold medieval coronet placed in the heart of every flower.

C. purpurea is purple-red in colour, and there are white and yellow species as well.

◁◁

Indoors in winter, or out a little later, there are few bulbs that give more spectacular display than the dazzling *Hippeastrum* hybrids, commonly sold as 'Royal Dutch Amaryllis'. These are the result of crossing many of seventy-five different *Hippeastrum* species, all from South America. Colours are limited to white and a full range of reds from pale orange to dark crimson, but these may be striped, splashed or graduated so that the variation appears wider, especially when combined with the natural gold and green throat markings. *Hippeastrum* bulbs are enormous, and should be potted up in winter with the bulb itself half out of the potting mix. Let them develop roots for about three weeks, then water, and like magic they'll push up great thick flower stems, fit to support the giant fiery flowers which may be all of nine inches in diameter. Sadly, they're almost scentless.

▷

Australia's most famous representative among the amaryllids is the startling 'Kangaroo Paw', one species of which is State flower of Western Australia. Something of a rarity in gardens of their own land, they are used for landscaping effect in Southern California, where they adore the dry winter. Their name *Anigosanthos* means 'expanding flower', for the individual blossoms split almost to the base as they open. The species *A. flavida* grows to six feet in height, and produces masses of furry flowers in combinations of brown, red, green and gold; their open starry throats are tinted a pale turquoise. The flowers last throughout the warm weather, gradually fading, never falling.

Ginger ~ ZÁZVOR
a dash of spice

'Who gave thee that jolly red nose?
Sinament and Ginger, Nutmeg and Cloves . . .'

We must thank seventeenth century poet Thomas Ravenscroft for that rollicking introduction to the stunning family of ginger flowers, the Zingiberaceae. Thomas lived in an age when fortunes were made and lost in the spice trade—when merchant adventurers ransacked the East for cargoes of hot and aromatic condiments that could be used to disguise the unpleasant flavours of gamy or pickled meats during the long European winters.

Cinnamon is the bark of a tree, nutmegs are a seed pod, cloves are a dried flower bud. Ginger is the plump tangy rhizome of a whole family of gorgeously flowering plants; though it is doubtful if Ravenscroft knew any of them beyond a kitchen acquaintance with their preserved or powdered roots.

The gingers are all decidedly tropical, from areas of the Pacific, Africa and particularly South East Asia, where they are valued as much for the decorative effect of their blossoms as for their production of the popular spice. There are 1250 species of them, all quite unfamiliar to cool-climate flower lovers who haven't had the good fortune to travel. Most send up tall succulent stems with canna-like leaves arranged spirally. The flowers appear from a series of bracts at the top of these stems, and quite often the bracts themselves are more startlingly coloured than the flowers, which generally open in the middle of the wet tropical summer.

In the case of the flaming Torch Ginger, stems may be twenty feet and more in height. Others vary widely down to the dwarf *Kaempferia* which rarely exceeds six inches. Showy variegated leaves are common among them, and entire flower stems are often cut for spectacular tropical arrangements. In the case of the fragrant *Hedychium*, individual blooms are pulled out of their bracts and worn in the hair or about the person.

◁
The Kahili Ginger (*Hedychium gardnerianum*) is probably the most commonly seen in a wide range of climates, for it is found up to an altitude of 8000 feet in the Himalayas, and is thus relatively cold resistant. The golden yellow butterfly flowers appear in a long spike at the top of a five-foot stem, and their eyecatching feature is a single lacquer-red stamen, longer than any other part of the flower. It is superbly fragrant and makes a splendid indoor decoration, lasting many days.

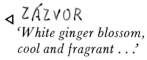

ᐊ ZÁZVOR
*'White ginger blossom,
cool and fragrant . . .'*

run the words of the old Hawaiian song—and this is the flower they sing about, *Hedychium coronarium*. Also known as the 'Garland Flower' or, to the Hawaiians *'Awapuhi-ke'oke'o'*, it is originally from India, where it is considered the most charming flower of all. The name *Hedychium* means 'Sweet Snow', a perfect description of the fragrant, satiny-white flower with just a touch of pastel yellow.

ᐊ

The Crepe or Malay Ginger is found over the entire Indo-Malaysian area as far north as the Philippines, but has also become naturalized in the American tropics. The translucent white and yellow blossoms appear one or two at a time from among the purplish red bracts. They have the texture of purest crepe silk. Its botanical name is *Costus speciosus*.

Alpinias form the largest group within the ginger family, about 250 species scattered from Africa, through India and Indonesia way out into the isles of Polynesia. *Alpinia speciosa*, or 'Shell Ginger' is popular for its dense foliage and the long clusters of red-tipped satiny pink flower buds, which open singly to reveal showy red and yellow flowers.

The 'Red Ginger' *Alpinia purpurata* is native to many island groups throughout the Pacific, where it may have come with the early Polynesian settlers. The actual flowers are white and inconspicuous, hardly noticeable among the profusion of bright red bracts which appear at the end of long stems.

The smaller *Alpinia calcarata* is found in India and southern China. It is an altogether daintier plant, with showy spikes of white blossom, tinted red and rosy-purple.

◁

Roscoeas are members of the
ginger family from high altitudes
of China and the Himalayas and
are thus more likely to be found
in cooler climate gardens than
other species. The Chinese
R. humeana produces showy
upright violet-purple flowers, in
appearance somewhere between
an iris and an orchid. Other
species flower in darker purple or
a butterscotch shade.

◁◁

Zingiber is the true ginger pro-
ducer of the ginger family; over
fifty species are found around the
Indonesian area. All are strictly
tropical and produce their flowers
on a separate stem from the
leaves. *Z. zerumbet* unveils a
dense spike of overlapping green
bracts. As these ripen to a rosy
red, the white star-shaped flowers
appear from among them, fragrant and marked in orange-yellow.
The species *Z. spectabile* is on the
whole showier, bearing a twenty-
four inch stem of looser scarlet
bracts which last for many
months. The small flowers are
white and pale yellow, with black
markings.

△
The Indonesian *Phaeomeria magnifica* or 'Torch Ginger' has become an outstanding feature in tropical gardens throughout the world. The glowing flower-head has an extraordinary coincidental likeness to the Australian waratah. Like that totally unrelated plant, it is actually a cone-shaped mass of bracts (in the case of *Phaeomeria* red, with white margins). The real flowers appear from among these; and several of them, scarlet with a gold edge, can be seen in our picture. The inflorescences of the Torch Ginger are approximately the size of a pineapple, which their fruit-cluster does indeed resemble. They are borne on five-foot stalks, the leaf stems developing separately to a height of twenty feet.

Down by the waterside

'*And this delightful Herb whose tender Green*
Fledges the River's Lip on which we lean—
Ah, lean upon it lightly! for who knows
From what once lovely Lip it springs unseen?'
                                    Omar Khayyam

Though they come from the four corners of the world and represent many unrelated botanical families, waterside plants are a race apart. They are a triumph of adaptation to their environment, which is a constant state of wetness. No danger of these beauties rotting in a boggy garden patch or fading when the water table rises after heavy rain. Most of them will even resist the violence of a sudden flash flood, for their roots spreading far and wide give them tremendous resistance. And afterward, they'll burst into growth in the newly deposited alluvial soil and mud. They are the real water babies, at home anywhere there is a constantly renewed water supply, or in lush riverside meadows prone to occasional flooding. Their seeds are carried by water and thrive anywhere the water deposits them.

All of them have a succulent juicy quality of stem and leaf structure, and heavy tuberous storage roots to guard against a sudden failure in supply of the precious element on which they depend.

Tropical waterside plants flower in summer when the rains appear; in temperate climates they prefer the early spring, a time of melting snows.

Their flowers are of many types, as our photographs reveal.

◁
Buttercups, *Primula, Lysichiton* and a variety of *Iris* thrive along the river's brink in the meadow garden of Wisley, the Royal Horticultural Society's garden in southern England. *Osmunda* fern and *Trollius* can also be seen.
UPOLÍN

◁
The waterside and bog gardens are always a popular exhibit at England's Chelsea Flower Show. Here is a prize-winning planting of *Mimulus, Astilbe, Dodecatheon* and *Primula japonica*, with *Iris, Acorus* and other moisture-loving plants for foliage effect.
KEJKLÍŘKA, ČECHRAVA, BOŽSKOKVĚT
PETRKLÍČ, KOSATEC,
PUŠKVOREC

125

ČECHRAVA

◁ The showy plumes of *Astilbe* are at their best in the cool, rich root-run of a waterside garden, preferably under the shade of riverside trees. The name *Astilbe* is from two Greek words meaning 'without brilliance', and make it clear the plant was named well before the gaily coloured modern hybrids were developed from Asiatic species. Its many popular names include 'Goat's Beard' and 'Meadowsweet'.

KYPREJ

▷ The old-fashioned 'Loosestrife', *Lythrum salicaria*, grows vigorously along the margins of streams all over the northern hemisphere and in Australia. The flower colour varies widely, but the best is a deep purple-red—the name '*Lythrum*' meaning stale blood.

VRBINA

▷ Showy free-flowering *Lysimachia*, the 'Yellow Loosestrife', is found wild in many parts of Europe and Asia, and was named for Lysimachus, an ancient king of Thrace. Smoke of the dried plant, when burned, is a primitive but effective insecticide, as an old verse by John Fletcher suggests:

> '. . . *Yellow Lysimachus, to give sweet rest*
> *To the faint shepherds, killing where it comes,*
> *All busy gnats, and every fly that hums.*'

Flies and gnats were apparently not its only victims, for the name was originally 'Louse-strife'!

◁ KOSATEC

Iris were named for the Greek goddess of the rainbow, and indeed there are modern hybrids in almost every imaginable shade. We are concerned, however, with the old waterside species like *Iris sibirica* which, in spite of its name, is from Europe, and probably the inspiration of the French royal emblem, the 'Fleur de Lys'.

▷ PRVOSENKA PETRKLÍČ

From the Italian *'Primaverola'*, meaning 'first flower of spring', we have taken our name *Primula*, and given it to some of the most decorative waterside plants in the world. *P. japonica*, the 'Candelabra Primrose', grows like a weed where the moisture level is high enough. Its variety 'Postford White' sends flower stems up as tall as three feet, producing layer upon layer of scented, snowy primrose flowers.

◁   KOSATEC

The Japanese Iris (*I. kaempferi*) has been in cultivation for several thousand years, and prefers to grow with its roots actually below water. Gardeners in Japan choose a position which can be flooded in the summer blooming season to produce the finest flowers. These are flat and triangular, and there are varieties in every imaginable combination of white, blue, purple, pink and crimson.

△
South African *Zantedeschias* or
'Calla Lilies', grow best in several
feet of water, their rhizomes
solidly anchored in the mud, well
out of reach of frost and cold
snaps. Like other members of the
arum family, its tiny flowers are
massed in the form of a spadix or
central column. This is surrounded by a colourful spathe or
ornamental leaf which may be
pink, white, crimson, orange or
yellow.

▷   UPOLÍN
Named from the German *'troll-
blume'*, *Trollius* are showy waterside relatives of the buttercups,
and like them, very free-flowering
for most of the year. The globe-
shaped flowers are spicily fragrant
and in many shades of yellow and
orange. It was believed that the
trolls, or wicked fairies, hid
poison in them to upset grazing
cows.

◁

The South American water-poppy, *Hydrocleys nymphoides* is neither a poppy nor a waterlily in spite of both its names and appearance. Useful for flooded areas in warm climates, it produces masses of floating, heart-shaped leaves and in warm weather long-stemmed golden flowers.

▷

KEJKLÍŘKA

The many colourful species of *Mimulus*, the Monkey Flower, are mostly from North America. They were once especially valued for their musky perfume, but this disappeared completely, world-wide, in 1914—no one knows why. We are left with their open cheerful monkey-faces in many bright colours. 'Whitecroft Scarlet' is a dwarf, waterloving species.

▽

Decorative in both leaf and spires of golden flowers, the tongue-twisting *Ligularia przewalski* romps in Asiatic water-meadows and beside overflowing ponds of European gardens. Curiously enough, it is classed as one of the daisies, (Compositae) although the family resemblance is hard to pick.

Orchids ~ lilies of the Tropics

'There are tropical lilies which are venomous, but they are more beautiful than the frail and icy-white lilies of the North.'

When the Irish-Greek writer Lafcadio Hearn wrote those lines, he was only echoing the general feeling of his time that there was something sinister about the strange and wonderful tropic orchids. Often the most glittering of them are found in the world's most inhospitable places—fever ridden jungles, treacherous swamps, slimy cliff-faces—yet they are most closely related to the *Liliums* of the cool northern hemisphere. Many do not, like normal plants, find nourishment in the earth, but have a pronounced affinity to decayed wood and rotting vegetation, clasping their thick, blunt-ended roots around other living matter and occasionally killing the host plant with their weight. In South America, they are known collectively as 'parasitos'—parasites.

If they have a perfume—and let's face it, few orchids are known for this quality—it is likely to be downright unpleasant or at best reminiscent of the faint sickly-sweet miasma of the hospital ward. So after all that—why do we still seek them out and lavish more time and trouble growing them than we do any other race of plants?

A brief glance at the following pages should answer that question more convincingly than mere words could ever do. What curious and remarkable creations!

There are over 15,000 natural orchid species, and infinitely more hybrids. Beautiful all of them, but in appearance so widely varied that it is difficult to understand how they could possibly be related, one to another. The secret is in the structure of the flowers themselves. All orchids have three outer petals (or sepals) arranged alternately with three true inner petals—never more or less. Of the three inner petals, one is invariably modified in some extraordinary way. It may be fringed or divided, hooded or cupped, enlarged or highly coloured. Sometimes it is formed with amazing vegetable mimicry to look like a bee, a butterfly, or any one of a number of things.

Orchids also have a different system of reproduction to other plants. Both male and female organs (instead of being separated as in other flowers) are contained in a single composite fleshy structure known as the *column*, which projects from the centre of the flower, often enfolded by the lip. Thus the lip acts as a lure or bait, attracting by its appearance not just any insect, but the particular type most adapted to efficient fertilization of the individual orchid flower.

As orchids produce unarguably the most exotic of flowers, it is something of a surprise to find that so many of them are among the

KATEYA - ORCHID

◁

As lovely a flower as you'll find anywhere, the exquisite hybrid 'Enid' is classed as a *Brasso-cattleya*, a man-made cross between the two orchid genera *Brassavola* and *Cattleya*, both from South America. Five inches across, it may bloom any time of year, and needs no artificial heating in a temperate climate.

toughest of plants. Often highly adaptable, they are not at all the temperamental and fussy hothouse beauties so many people imagine.

Of those illustrated, *Coelogyne*, *Cymbidium* and *Paphiopedilum* can be grown potted in the open garden or on a terrace in any frost-free position outside the tropics. The others will mostly do well if you can give them a winter minimum of around 50° F (10°C). Often a kitchen or bathroom makes a quite satisfactory location in the cooler months.

Both plants and cut flowers of the *Cattleya* group are expensive to buy because they are slow growing, normally producing only one new flower stem per year. But that flower will stay in perfect condition for weeks. Most of the spectacular *Cattleyas* one sees are in fact crosses between two or more of four orchidaceous genera, *Brassavola*, *Cattleya*, *Laelia* and *Sophronitis*, all from South America.

△
The exact parentage of this stunning lime-yellow *Cattleya* is unknown, but an educated guess would suggest that its scarlet lip could be traced to some *Brassavola* parentage. The multiple flowering habit is common to many of the South American *Cattleyas*.

ORCHIDSE

▷
'Chine Bouton d'Or' (or Chinese Gold Button) is the name given to this wonderful *Cattleya* cross. Probably it achieves its golden colour from a *Laelia* ancestor; certainly nothing quite like it is found in nature.

▷
At England's Chelsea Flower Show, one of the most eyecatching exhibits is always the mass display of *Cattleya* hybrids, arranged in waves of a particular colour. Here among the cheerful deep pinks is an enormous-flowered hybrid between the *Brassocattleya* '*Nigiana*' and the *Laeliocattleya* '*Kathleen Jeal*'.

Cymbidium ORCHIDEA

These hardy orchids are the types most commonly seen in florist shops everywhere, and also the most widely grown outdoors in temperate climates. Well grown plants of good varieties may produce long arching flower sprays up to five feet in length, each consisting of twenty-five or more four-inch blooms. These may be of any shade short of the blues and mauves. The parentage of hybrid *Cymbidiums* is very complex, including many species from South East Asia and Australia. They flower from mid-winter on. The name *Cymbidium* is from the Greek '*kymbe*' (a foot), referring to the shape of the flower lip.

▷
This delicately coloured hybrid reveals the superb texture and elegant shape that have brought *Cymbidiums* such popularity as a corsage flower. Australia alone exports millions of blooms every year.

◁
Australian and Californian flower-lovers take for granted sights like this—a great arching spray of *Cymbidium* in full bloom in the open garden. In cooler areas, though, it is better to bring them indoors until danger of frost is past.

▷
Cymbidium 'Sensation' var. *Prunus*, is a showy brick-red hybrid with a blotched lip and striped petals. Its rounded fuller shape was indeed something of a sensation among orchid breeders.

◁

With a little imagination, one can see why these showy orchids were named *Coelogyne,* a hodgepodge of Greek and Latin words meaning 'heavenly woman' or 'angel'. At any rate, the snowy angel wings and golden haloed throat are a sight of unearthly beauty in the early spring.

▷

Two Greek words *'dendron'* (a tree) and *'bios'* (life) have been adapted to name the remarkable orchid genus *Dendrobium* or tree-livers. More than a thousand species have been discovered all over Asia and out into the Pacific. Generally they bear long arching sprays of flowers from the top of a stick-like pseudobulb. The illustrated variety is a hybrid of Queensland's State flower, the 'Cooktown Orchid'.

◁

Simple and somewhat ascetic in appearance, the Central American orchid *Lycaste* is often known as the 'White Nun', possibly because of the arrangement of the three petals, which may resemble a nun's headdress. These are in the centre of the flower, while the three elongated appendages are the protective sepals, which give *Lycaste virginalis* a rather triangular appearance.

◁
Named for a once-famous collector of exotic plants, Viscount Milton; the appealing *Miltonias* are more commonly known as Pansy Orchids, for obvious reasons. The twenty-odd species have a fairly limited spectrum of crimson, brown, pink and white, but so variously are they patterned that the range seems almost endless. The illustrated variety is 'Mrs J. B. Crow'.

The Slipper Orchids

STŘEVÍČNÍK
PANTOFLÍČEK

The 'Slipper Orchids' are largely
terrestrial and found on many
continents. At one stage, they
were all called *Cypripedium* or
'Venus Slipper' after the earliest
known wild European types. But
gradually, taxonomists recognized important differences in the
look-alike species from other continents, so they were renamed,
though often retaining a verbal
link with the old goddess for
whom the original genus was
named.

The *Paphiopedilums*, for instance,
are named for *Paphos*, an ancient
city sacred to Venus; and the
tropical Nepalese species illustrated at left has been named for
the goddess herself *P. venustum*.
The recognizable feature of all
species is the deep lip which
resembles the toe of a slipper. In
the case of *Phragmipedilums*, the
other two petals have also been
developed into long, tail-like
appendages.

Credits

The flowers posed for my camera in Australia, Czechoslovakia, England, France, Hawaii, Hong Kong, Japan, Moorea, Ra'iatea, Samoa, Tahiti, the United States.

My distinguished assistants, drivers and navigators included: Bugs and Joanna Burley, Horace Clay, Louise Coleman, Lex Dampier, Brian Donges, Bill, Ruth and Owen Farrior, David Garde, Dave and Barbara Goux, Michel Hello, James Hodgson, Milton I, Betty Klein, James Lichtman, Bruce McKillop, Milton Meyer, Richard Moody, Colin Olson, Damien Parer, Jacques Rentier, Coco Teamo, Glenn Thompson, Arnaud de Vinzelles and John Winston.

All pictures were taken on Kodak Ektachrome, using a Rollei SL 66 and a Nikon F2.

◁ ORCHID

Fascinating rather than spectacular, the flowers of the orchid genus *Arpophylla* are very small indeed, but borne in incredibly large numbers all along the length of a crowded two-foot spike. Each flower is a perfect miniature of better known hothouse types. The name *Arpophylla* means 'Scimitar-leaf' and the species *A. gigantea* is from Mexico. The flower spike is very long lasting.

Index to pictures

Botanical and popular names are in alphabetical order.
Botanical names are in *italics*.

'One thing is certain, and
 the Rest is Lies;
The Flower that once has
 blown for ever dies!
 Omar Khayyam

Rosa sarmentosa 'Golden Wings'